£6.95

THE BROWN RICE COOKBOOK

Brown rice is more than just nutritious – it is delicious, with a flavour white rice cannot match. Here is information, advice and a wide range of varied recipes to help you make full use of this wholesome healthfood.

D0823874

Also by Craig Sams:
ABOUT MACROBIOTICS

THE BROWN RICE COOKBOOK

A Selection of
Delicious Wholesome Recipes

by

CRAIG and ANN SAMS

Illustrated by Clive Birch

THORSONS PUBLISHERS LIMITED
Wellingborough, Northamptonshire

First published 1980
Fifth Impression 1982

© CRAIG and ANN SAMS 1980

*This book is sold subject to the condition that it shall not, by way of trade or
otherwise, be lent, re-sold, hired out, or otherwise circulated without the
publisher's prior consent in any form of binding or cover other than that in
which it is published and without a similar condition including this
condition being imposed on the subsequent purchaser.*

British Library Cataloguing in Publication Data

Sams, Craig
    The brown rice cookbook.
    1. Cookery (Rice)
    2. Rice, Unpolished
    I. Title II. Sams, Ann
    641.6'3'18   TX809.R5

    ISBN 0-7225-0642-2
    ISBN 0-7225-0610-4 Pbk

Printed and bound in Great Britain

CONTENTS

Liquid Measure Equivalents

British	American
1 teaspoonful	$1\frac{1}{4}$ teaspoonsful
1 tablespoonful	$1\frac{1}{4}$ tablespoonsful
1 pint (20 fl oz)	$1\frac{1}{4}$ pints

Cup Measures

A British standard measuring cupful contains 10 fl oz (275ml).

An American standard measuring cupful contains 8 fl oz (225ml).

INTRODUCTION

Recent years have seen a great increase in the consumption and availability of brown rice. Whereas white rice was once the only variety known, brown rice now enjoys widespread popularity not only among dedicated healthfood users but also with many cooks who use it as a flavoursome ingredient in their culinary repertoire.

In the early 1960's many people in Europe and the U.S.A. were attracted to the ideas of Georges Ohsawa, a Japanese who had rediscovered the importance of dietary balance in traditional Eastern medicine. Guided by the principle that digestive health underpins the total condition of the body he taught macrobiotics, a dietary system in which brown rice plays a major role. With the general awakening of interest in Eastern ideas and with the increase in awareness of bodily health brown rice and associated foods became more widely used. In the world of pop music the expression 'brown rice sandwiches' was used in association with the musicians who adopted wholefood diets. Then in the mid-1970's came the bran boom with an upsurge in demand for wholewheat bread, brown rice, pop corn and beans. In fact anything with that magic ingredient – 'dietary fibre' – was hailed by orthodox medicine as the cure for all kinds of bodily ills. The decline in consumption of white bread is now paralleled by a decrease in white sugar consumption, the first in peacetime in a century, as a new awareness of the importance of diet to health develops.

Brown rice is more than just nutritious – it is delicious, with a full, nutty flavour that white rice can never match. It is versatile, enhancing a wide variety of other foods in infinite combinations. Why, then, did brown rice ever lose its once pre-eminent position to white rice? The answer lies partly in the fact that while white rice will keep almost indefinitely, brown rice should be fresh. It attracts insects once it has been husked, so it needs more care in storage and more attention to efficient distribution.

In the nineteenth and early twentieth century it was economically convenient to have rice in a form that was easily stored, quickly cooked, and long-lasting. Even today the extra attention that handling brown rice requires means that it sells at a higher price, even though it has not been processed as much as white rice. Also, brown rice of poor quality is visibly less attractive. Polishing conceals a multitude of faults. Powdered talc and glucose are also frequently dusted over white rice to enhance its appearance, so if you do use white rice it is a good idea to wash it thoroughly before preparation.

Most of the recipes in this book will work with different varieties of rice, or with mixtures of more than one kind.

1
VARIETIES OF RICE

Rice is believed to have originally been grown from wild plants that thrived in Indonesia and South-East Asia. Now it is to be found on every continent, growing in a wide variety of climates and conditions. The numerous varieties of rice that exist are an indication of both regional taste and geographical differences. The main mode of classification of rice is by the size of the grain: short, medium, or long.

Short Grain

Short grain rice grains are about 5mm in length and have a soft texture when cooked. Commonly used in puddings, short grain rice has a wide variety of savoury uses and is particularly good when served with sauces or with vegetables. It can be served with an ice-cream scoop. A slightly glutinous strain of short grain rice is cultivated in Japan and is being grown increasingly in Italy, France, Spain, and California in response to demand for this variety from brown rice eaters.

Medium Grain

Medium grain rice is similar to short grain but longer, about 6mm. Grown in Italy and the U.S.A. its appeal is mainly in the form of white rice, although in its brown form it is absorbent and used in dishes with yogurt or vegetables sauces.

Long Grain

Long grain rice is slender in shape and can be from 6-8mm in length. The grains are dry when cooked and do not stick to each other. The best varieties of long grain rice are grown in sub-tropical climates, particularly Texas, Surinam, and Thailand.

Similar to Long Grain rice in thinness but shorter and somewhat chewier in texture are Basmati rice and California long grain rice.

Sweet Brown Rice

Sweet brown rice is a very glutinous variety originating from Japan. Its sweet flavour and moist texture when cooked make it ideal for desserts where one wishes to keep sweeteners to a minimum, and also as an addition to some other variety of rice being cooked.

Red Rice

This grows in South-East Asia and is similar to long grain in shape. Because it is hardy it is grown where other rice crops would not thrive. It is dull in colour when polished so generally the whole grains are eaten by poorer people or used as animal feed. A purplish-black long grain variety is grown in China and can sometimes be found in Chinese grocers. Green grains may appear in some varieties of brown rice, particularly from France and Italy. These are fully-ripened grains which have not had sufficient sunshine during their final ripening to turn a golden-brown colour. Once cooked, these grains are similar to the browner grains in every respect.

White Rice

Almost any of the above varieties of rice can be turned into white rice by the removal of the bran layers of the grain and the germ to leave the starchy white kernel. The bran and germ contain almost all the vitamins and minerals and oils of the grain, as well as much of the protein.

The main disadvantages of using white rice, apart from the loss of nutritive elements comes from the loss of the high-fibre bran layers of the grain. The effect of consuming bran is twofold: firstly, the appetite is satisfied at a reasonable level – a feeling of fullness arises due to the very bulk of the bran and overeating leading to obesity is less likely to occur. Secondly, the fibre element helps speed and facilitate the digestive process thereby reducing the likelihood of diseases of the intestine.

Parboiled Rice

Sometimes called 'brown' rice, this is a processed rice that is the result of an attempt to avoid the worst effects of rice-milling. The whole unhusked grains of rice are immersed in hot water and some of the B-vitamins and soluble minerals in the bran and germ soak into the starchy kernel. The grains are then dried and the bran and germ are removed. The result is a rice that has a dull brown colour, a little flavour, and just enough vitamins to keep the consumer from developing beri-beri or pellagra, two diseases that arise directly from the refining of rice where it is a staple part of the diet.

Wild Rice

Wild rice is not really a member of the family of the other rices but is an aquatic grass whose large dark grains stand on long stalks in the lakes of Canada and North Central United States. The grains are harvested by threshing the heads of the plants against the inside hull of a canoe. Wild rice is expensive, but a little mixed with long grain rice before cooking can have a considerable effect.

2
CHOOSING YOUR INGREDIENTS

Rice and Beans

Brown rice is rich in a wide variety of essential amino acids, the constituent proteins needed for tissue development and growth. Combined with the members of the bean family, which contain other amino acids, one obtains a range of amino acids that exceeds the constituents of either of the foods taken separately. This effect, known as synergy, applies to other combinations of cereals and pulses, such as bread and lentil soup.

To get the full benefit of this synergistic effect, the rice and beans should be eaten at the same meal. In general, however, they cannot be cooked together, although there are some exceptions, i.e. pre-soaked adzuki beans can be cooked with rice together in a pressure cooker – the cooking periods are the same for both.

Soaking beans for at least twelve hours is a very important aspect of the preparation process: not only are the beans easier to cook to a soft consistency, but in the soaking period the dormant life force of the bean is activated, and it begins the changes that will in a few days lead to sprouting and the development of roots, stalk and leaves.

This little change makes a great difference to the digestibility and the nutrient availability of the cooked bean – it is no good eating a food because a laboratory analysis shows that it is rich in protein if it gives you indigestion, flatulence and your digestive system only extracts a small part of the available nutritional content.

Pythagoras would not let his students eat beans because he believed they inhibited the higher intellectual processes. However, it is likely that this was because the prevalent bean of classical Greece was the fava bean – harmless in itself but with a hard brown skin which, if regularly eaten can lead to favism, symptoms of which are deterioration of vision and mental faculties. Foods such as adzuki beans, chickpeas, lentils, and black soybeans in particular, when properly cooked, can only enhance the functioning of mind and body.

Vegetables

As with grains and beans, vegetables are that much better when organically grown. The advantages of eating foods that do not contain either external residues of insecticides or internal traces of systemic herbicides need little elaboration. Agricultural chemicals are particularly damaging to the body's cleansing organs like the kidneys and liver, and they accumulate in the body's fat reserves, storing future harm. It takes several generations for the human body to adapt to environmental changes, small consolation if you are exposing yourself to them now.

Soya Sauce

Soya sauce is a name that covers a multitude of brown seasonings. At one end of the spectrum is the manufactured soya sauce containing hydrolyzed vegetable proteins, caramel colouring, monosodium glutamate, salt, and water. Real soya sauce or *shoyu* is a naturally fermented product made from a broth of soyabeans and wheat, carefully matured for over a year. *Tamari* soya sauce is also fermented, from soyabeans alone, and has a rich savoury flavour. The glutamic acid that derives from the soyabeans used is not only a flavour enhancer but also a valuable amino acid, or basic protein.

Miso soya bean *purée* is made from soyabeans and various cereals and is a paste similar in flavour to soya sauce. It is also naturally fermented over a long period. From Japan, the most popular variety is *genmai miso* which is made from brown rice and soyabeans and has a savoury/sweet flavour with none of the bitterness of some *misos*.

Oil

As with white rice, popular tastes in a food to some extent reflects the most convenient form from the food manufacturer's or processor's point of view. Refined oils have no flavour of their own, and store well with the addition of a small amount of antioxidant chemicals. Unrefined oils have distinctive flavours, of which olive oil is best-known, and have a higher level of free fatty acids which can lead eventually to rancidity in old or badly stored oils. Fresh unrefined oils extracted without solvent chemicals make an incomparable difference to dishes in which they are used.

Seaweeds and Wild Vegetables

These can, when used in small quantities, provide trace elements that the body needs and which are lacking in foods grown in regularly cultivated ground. *Kombu, wakame,* and *arame* from Japan, as well as dulse from Ireland, provide piquant tastes that harmonize with most foods. Wild vegetables such as nettles and fat hen can be used with, or in place of, spinach where greens are called for. Chickweed is good in salads, and young burdock roots are quite a good substitute for other root vegetables.

Sugar

Sugar is not included in any of the recipes that follow. Dried fruits, concentrated fruit juices, or malt extract all provide sweetness that does not have the same unbalancing effect on the blood-sugar levels as cane or beet sugars and glucose. The over-consumption of refined sugars not only leads to obesity and disease but also undermines one's sense of taste and ability to enjoy the less pronounced sweetness that is present in other foods.

Salt

Sea salt is preferred because, being unrefined, it contains not only sodium chloride but many valuable trace minerals as well. Natural crystal salt, mined in Cheshire, can be obtained unrefined in health food shops and many supermarkets and derives from a sea that dried up in prehistoric times – it has all the qualities of sea salt.

Dried Fruit

Whenever possible dried fruit that has not been treated with sulphur dioxide should be used as it has more flavour and sweetness. Raisins and sultanas are frequently treated with liquid paraffin. This assists cake manufacturers and fruit packers as the fruit flows freely and does not stick together, but is hardly necessary for domestic use.

Kitchen Utensils

All kitchen utensils should be made of non-reactive materials like stainless steel or glass. Aluminium can impart off flavours and colours, enamel pans chip, and cast-iron is best used for frying rather than boiling. The extra cost in obtaining stainless steel serving spoons is repaid by their longer usable life. Many plated utensils soon lose their outer finish and this goes straight into your food.

3
COOKING
BROWN RICE

Most of the recipes in this book call for pre-cooked rice. There are a variety of methods for preparing the uncooked grains, and you may find that you will want to vary the cooking times, salt levels, or proportion of water used to suit your personal taste.

Boiled Brown Rice

Always check your rice for the presence of any foreign bodies; a small stone or other particle can spoil someone's enjoyment of an entire meal. There is no pre-cleaning method that is 100 per cent effective, so the extra precaution of picking over your rice is worth the minute or two it may take.

Then wash your rice. You can simply place the saucepan under a running tap and let the water flow over the top, or shake it in water in a closed container and then pour away the water through a strainer, either way you get rid of dust and dirt that may detract from the flavour of the rice.

1 cupful brown rice
2 cupsful water
¼ teaspoonful salt

Bring the water to the boil and allow to boil for three minutes. Reduce heat to lowest possible level and simmer, covered, for 40 minutes to one hour or until water has all been absorbed and rice is just beginning to scorch. Remove from heat, stir, let stand for five minutes, and it is ready to serve. Do not stir rice while it is cooking.

Pressure-cooked Brown Rice

Because there is less evaporation you can use less water when pressure-cooking rice. For larger quantities you can reduce the proportion of water used from that given below.

**1 cupful brown rice
1¼ cupsful water
¼-½ teaspoonful salt**

Bring combined ingredients to full pressure, then lower heat and cook for 35-45 minutes. Remove from heat and let stand for at least ten minutes. Remove cover, mix rice, and serve.

Baked Brown Rice

**2 cupsful brown rice
3-3½ cupsful water
½ teaspoonful salt**

For an extra nutty flavour stir the rice in a dry frying pan on top of the cooker until it is warm and becomes a golden brown. Place in a covered casserole with the water and salt and bake for 45 minutes in a 350°F/180°C (Gas Mark 4) oven. Remove and allow to cool a bit before serving as it is much hotter straight from the pan than boiled rice.

Steamed Brown Rice

Left-over cooked brown rice can be steamed to reheat it before use. It is also possible to obtain tender fluffy rice using the following method. This is particularly recommended for long grain rice.

4 cupsful water
1¼ cupsful brown rice
1¼ teaspoonsful salt

Sprinkle the rice into the boiling water and add the salt. When all the rice is added stir for a moment and boil for 10-15 minutes. The grains should be tender but still brittle in the middle. Rinse the grains in hot water and then wrap in a tea towel or cheesecloth and steam in a colander or steamer for about thirty minutes.

Variations
Add *tamari* or *shoyu* soya sauce to the rice instead of salt. A few *sautéed* vegetables such as onions or celery can be added to the rice when cooking. Dried chestnuts, with two parts of water extra added, impart their sweet flavour to cooking rice. Alternatively, add a small proportion of uncooked barley, rye, or wheat to the rice. For extra tenderness, pre-soak these grains before adding.

If you have a temperature control that will enable you to bake at a low temperature, baked rice can be made overnight, using the same recipe as above but cooking at a lower temperature. The scorched and yellowish rice at the bottom of the pan can be removed by sprinkling it with water and reheating the pan for a few minutes. This rice is very tasty and chewy, and delicious dipped in a mixture of soya sauce, ginger and chopped green onions.

Rice Cream Cereal

Purée cooked brown rice with extra water and cook to a soft mushy consistency. The resulting cereal can be seasoned to taste for a breakfast cereal, and for invalids or infants.

Popped Rice

Popped brown rice is not a light fluffy product like pop corn, but it is deliciously crunchy and the pre-soaking period enhances the sweetness of the grains. Once you have popped your rice it can be stored for several weeks in an airtight jar or even a thick polythene bag, tightly sealed and kept in the fridge, to be used as required.

Try oven-toasting pumpkin seeds, sesame seeds or sunflower seeds, then lightly sprinkle them with natural soya sauce, and mix with popped rice. You will have a delicious snack that is irresistible to children and adults alike and, because of the chewing it requires, provides excellent exercise for the teeth and gums.

To pop brown rice:
Soak two cupsful of rice in water – enough to cover well. Leave overnight then change water daily for three more days. Finally rinse well and empty rice to about half-inch depth into a heavy bottomed skillet over medium heat, stirring constantly until rice is popped and brown. Remove from skillet and season with soya sauce while still hot.

4
RICE AND VEGETABLES

This classic dish serves as a nutritious vegetarian staple meal and, despite the limitations implied by its title, the permutations are infinite. In his reflections on childhood days, Mao Tse Tung, remarkably, failed to moralize on the advantages or disadvantages of this diet. He merely remarked that his father, an ambitious middle peasant, turned his livestock into cash at the local market, and restricted young Mao to a diet of coarse unpolished rice and vegetables, with fish on rare occasions. While the diet no doubt did him nothing but good, who knows what rebellious resentment of the profit motive developed in his mind as he watched the live produce of his father's farm being trotted off to grace other people's tables.

Rice and Carrots

This is a quick and easy-to-prepare dish. When I first developed an appetite for regular helpings of brown rice, this featured so regularly on my menu that I later abandoned it altogether, to rediscover it with pleasure nearly fifteen years later for inclusion here.

Grate one pound (450g) of washed carrots on a coarse grater. *Sauté* grated carrots in a frying pan in two tablespoonsful of oil until the oil begins to acquire an orange tinge, then add three tablespoonsful of sesame seeds and *sauté* further until carrots are soft through. Serve as a bed for, or on a bed of, freshly boiled or steamed left-over brown rice.

Mushroom Fried Rice

2 cupsful cooked long grain rice
1 chopped onion
1 cupful sliced mushrooms
oil
soya sauce

Sauté onions for five minutes, add mushrooms and cook until mushrooms are tender and cooked through. Add the cooked rice and stir and fry for another two to three minutes adding soya sauce to taste. Serve garnished with chopped parsley.

Fried Rice and Vegetables

1 teaspoonful soya sauce
2 cupsful pre-cooked rice
1 carrot
1 onion
1 swede
1 cupful bean sprouts
¼ lb frozen peas
4 cloves of garlic
1 teaspoonful ground cumin
1 tablespoonful sesame oil

Use heavy skillet. Heat oil. *Sauté* onions and garlic. Add cumin. Then add carrots and swedes. Finally add sprouts and peas. Cook over high heat stirring constantly. Add rice and soya sauce and heat for further five minutes.

Bananas and Rice

Throughout Latin America and South-East Asia, bananas are frequently used with rice, not for desserts but as a main meal. The original bananas are known as plantains, although green in colour, are highly nutritious. Most bananas nowadays are the sweet yellow variety which, although higher in natural sugar content and lower in other nutritive qualities, cause little harm except in some of the producing countries where the natives have unwittingly substituted them for the plantain as their principal food.

3 cupsful cooked long grain brown rice
2 onions, chopped
vegetable oil
soya sauce
4 eggs
4 bananas

Sauté the onions in oil until soft. Add the cooked brown rice and heat together, seasoning with soya sauce. Fry the eggs in another pan 'sunnyside up'.

Place the onion-rice mixture on individual plates, and form a pit in the middle. Fill the pit with one fried egg. Slice the bananas lengthwise and fry in the oil in which the eggs have been fried. When they are slightly browned at the edges, remove and place the strips of banana on the rice around the pit containing the egg.

Garnish with parsley or strips of raw carrot and serve. This recipe serves four.

Rice and Green Herbs

**2 cupsful brown rice
1 cupful pre-cooked chopped spinach
8 spring onions
2 heaped tablespoonsful chopped mixed
rosemary, thyme, majoram, tarragon, summer
savory
½ teaspoonful black peppercorns
1 or 2 cloves garlic
1 teaspoonful grated lemon rind
1 teaspoonful lemon juice
2 teaspoonsful sunflower seed oil
1 teaspoonful salt**

Cook the rice until done, then let it cool. Chop the spinach with the spring onions, combine with herbs and lemon rind and mix into the rice. Crush the salt, garlic and peppercorns together and mix with the rice. Cover and leave for ten minutes for the flavours to blend. Before serving sprinkle with lemon juice and the oil.

This recipe can vary enormously depending on the herbs you use. We sometimes add chopped rue for a strong bitter pungent quality, and it is also delicious with a predominating fresh basil flavour, perhaps lightly sprinkled with crumbs of Caerphilly cheese.

Almond Rice

Try to use Jordan as opposed to Californian almonds in this recipe, for their extra flavour. You can substitute cashews, whole or broken, or hazels.

2 cupsful cooked brown rice
1 clove garlic
1 tablespoonful chopped parsley
½\tablespoonful dried marjoram and thyme
½ cupful almonds which have been oven-roasted
until lightly browned in centre

As soon as the rice has finished cooking, stir in the almonds and herbs, cover and let stand for ten minutes.

Rice and Cauliflower

2 tablespoonsful oil
1½ cupsful rice
1 large cauliflower
1 large onion, chopped
3 cupsful boiling water
1 large tub plain yogurt (cow or goat)

Sauté rice in oil for a few minutes in a large heavy saucepan. Add three cupsful of boiling water then turn down heat to a gentle simmer. *Sauté* cauliflower gently for a few minutes. *Sauté* onion gently for a few minutes. Lay both on top of rice. Cover with lid. Cook for 45 minutes over gentle heat and then serve with yogurt in side dish.

Rice Rissoles

3 cupsful cooked rice
¼ cupful finely chopped parsley
1 pinch salt
1 cupful sautéed onions
½ cupful roasted sunflower seeds
1 cupful béchamel sauce
1 tablespoonful oil
3 chopped spring onions

Mix together, binding with béchamel sauce. Shape into patties using plain flour and fry in pan.

Moroccan Rice Alicantina

4 tablespoonsful oil
3-4 crushed cloves garlic
3 large green peppers, sliced
1 cupful artichoke hearts
3 large tomatoes, chopped
1 cupful green beans, chopped
1½ cupsful rice, long grain
¼ teaspoonful salt
pinch black pepper
pinch turmeric
3 pints (1.7 litres) vegetable stock or water

Fry the garlic in hot oil with sliced green peppers. Set aside. *Sauté* artichokes, chopped tomatoes and chopped beans. Add rice, seasonings and turmeric. Stir in the 3 pints (1.7 litres) of stock. Simmer briskly for ten minutes stirring constantly. Then simmer gently until rice is cooked (approx. another 30 minutes). Stand to one side of the stove and allow to dry out. Then stir in garlic and green pepper mixture. Serve warm.

Zen Hash

This dish was featured on the menu of the Zen Hashery, one of New York's earliest macrobiotic restaurants.

2 lbs (900g) courgettes
1 lb (450g) spinach
1 large onion
1 carrot
½ cupful soya sauce
½ cupful pine kernels or cashew bits
4 tablespoonsful oil
cooked brown rice

Quarter and slice courgettes. Coarsely chop spinach and onions. Grate carrot. In a large frying pan, *sauté* onions until golden in colour. Add courgettes and *sauté* until nearly done (about five minutes). Add soya sauce and nuts. Mix well, then add carrots and spinach and cook for another three to five minutes until spinach is done. Season to taste. Place brown rice on plates with hollowed out beds in the middle to fill with the vegetable mixture. Garnish with parsley sprigs, carrot sticks or whole radishes (including tops).

Spring Risotto

4 tablespoonsful olive oil
1 onion, chopped
2 cupsful long grain brown rice
3¼ cupsful water, boiling
2 leeks, chopped
1 small cauliflower
1 lb (450g) broccoli (heads only)
¼ lb (225g) spinach, chopped
¼ lb (225g) strong cheddar cheese
1 tablespoonful butter
Salt, pepper and cayenne
4 spring onions, finely chopped

Heat two tablespoonsful of olive oil in a heavy saucepan and *sauté* onion for five minutes. Then add the rice, stirring well to coat all the grains in oil. Add the boiling water and a pinch of salt. Cover and simmer for 40 minutes.

Heat the remaining two tablespoonsful of oil in a heavy casserole. *Sauté* the cauliflower, broccoli, leeks and seasonings together, stirring gently for about ten minutes. Then add the spinach, stirring for a few minutes whilst it reduces in size. Add the cooked rice and half the cheese. Sprinkle the remaining cheese and the cayenne on top and grill till the cheese is melted and golden. Sprinkle with the spring onions and serve.

Stuffed Vine Leaves

½ lb (225g) vine leaves
¾ cupful cooked rice
¼ chopped tomato
1 teaspoonful salt
½ cupful parsley, finely chopped
¼ cupful chopped pine nuts
1¼ cupsful water or vegetable stock
3 or 4 crushed cloves garlic
4 tablespoonsful lemon juice
2 teaspoonsful of dried mint

Dip vine leaves a few at a time in boiling water. Prepare filling by mixing rice, chopped tomato, pine nuts, parsley, mint, seasoning and ¼ cupful of the stock. Place 1 teaspoonful of the mixture in the centre of a leaf. Fold tip of leaf and the stem end of leaf towards centre. Fold sides in toward centre then roll leaf gently to give a torpedo shape. Lay rolled leaves neatly in a pan. Add 1 cupful of stock. Sprinkle with lemon juice and seasoning. Cover with a plate to prevent movement. Simmer gently for 1 hour. Drain off remaining stock and mix with crushed garlic. Pour over vine leaves and simmer for a few more minutes. Serve hot with the sauce or cold sprinkled with lemon juice.

Brown Rice with Grapes and Pine Nuts

2 tablespoonsful olive oil
1 large onion, chopped
2 oz (50g) pine nuts
1¼ cupsful long grain brown rice
1½ cupsful vegetable stock or water, boiling
½ teaspoonful thyme
1 bayleaf
¾ lb (350g) black grapes, peeled, halved and seeded
salt and pepper

Heat oil in a heavy saucepan. *Sauté* onion until soft and golden. Add pine nuts and cook until they are lightly browned also. Add the rice, stirring well until the grains are well coated with oil. Add the stock, bring to the boil then add the thyme and bayleaf. Cover the pan and simmer gently until the rice is tender (approx. 45 minutes) and has absorbed the stock. Season with the salt and pepper. Add the grapes. Do not cook any further but allow the grapes to warm through only. Delicious served with a vegetable casserole.

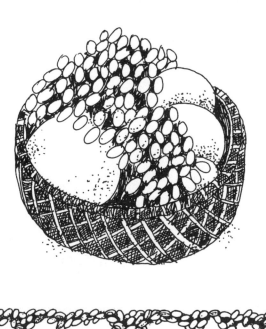

5
BROWN RICE AND SAUCES

In whatever company it is served, boiled or baked brown rice benefits from the addition of some kind of sauce. In its simplest form this may just be a dash of soya sauce or a few spoonsful of the juices from a vegetable dish. Some of the more elaborate sauces practically make a meal on their own when combined with rice.

Vegetable Sauce

1 tablespoonful oil
1 onion, thinly sliced
1 green pepper, thinly sliced
1 carrot, thinly sliced
3 cloves garlic, finely chopped
¾ cupful water
3 tablespoonsful soya sauce, *tamari* **or** *shoyu*
1-1½ tablespoonsful *kuzu* **powder, dissolved in a little cold water**
2 teaspoonsful ginger, freshly grated

Heat the oil in a heavy bottomed skillet or pan and *sauté* the vegetables and garlic until they are tender. Add the water and the soya sauce and bring to the boil. Stir in the dissolved *kuzu* (if unobtainable, use arrowroot instead) and the grated ginger and simmer, stirring constantly for about one minute or until the sauce thickens and is transparent. If you cannot get fresh ginger, use powdered instead.

There are many different vegetables you can use in this sauce. Oriental chefs often use Lotus roots, Daikow (large white radish), Chinese cabbage, mushrooms, beansprouts, cauliflower or white cabbage.

Sweet and Sour Sauce

1 tablespoonful oil
1 onion, thinly sliced
½ carrot, chopped finely
1 green pepper, chopped finely
1 cupful water
2 tablespoonsful soya sauce
4 teaspoonsful honey
2 teaspoonsful vinegar (preferably rice)
2 teaspoonsful *kuzu*, dissolved in a little water

Heat a heavy bottomed pan and *sauté* the vegetables in the oil for five minutes. Add the water, soya sauce, honey and vinegar and bring to the boil, then simmer gently for another five minutes. Stir in the dissolved *kuzu* and cook gently until thickened.

Sesame Sauce

1 teaspoonful *kuzu* powder, dissolved in a little water
1 cupful water
1 tablespoonful hatcho miso (soya paste)
1 teaspoonful *tahini* (sesame paste)
1 teaspoonful ginger, freshly grated or powdered

Add the *kuzu* powder (ready dissolved) into the cupful of water in a saucepan. Bring to the boil and then simmer for a few minutes until the sauce has thickened. Mix in the remaining ingredients and simmer for a few more minutes.

Delicious served over steamed cauliflower, asparagus, potatoes, broccoli or any *sautéed* vegetables.

Apple Dessert Sauce

1½ tablespoonsful *kuzu*
1 tablespoonful honey
a cupful apple concentrate
½ cupful water
1 tablespoonful lemon juice
¼ teaspoonful nutmeg

Combine the *kuzu*, honey and half a cupful of apple concentrate in a pan mixing well. Stir in the remaining apple juice and water. Bring to the boil stirring constantly until the sauce has thickened. Stir in the lemon juice and nutmeg. Serve hot or cold over fruits or rice pudding.

is for apple

Basic Onion Sauce

4 tablespoonsful oil
4 tablespoonsful wholewheat flour
1 cupful water
3 tablespoonsful chopped onion
1 clove garlic, crushed
soya sauce

Sauté onion and garlic in oil for a few minutes, until onions become translucent. Add flour and stir whilst frying for another minute. Add the water slowly, stirring constantly to ensure lumps do not form. When the sauce has thickened, season to taste with soya sauce.

This sauce can benefit from the following additions once you have prepared the basic sauce.

Mustard Sauce
Add one teaspoonful of powdered mustard and one tablespoonful of lemon juice to the onion sauce.

Dill and Yogurt Sauce
Add two teaspoonsful of dried dill (leaves or seeds) and four tablespoonsful of yogurt to the completed sauce.

Egg Sauce
Add two chopped hard boiled eggs.

Miso Sauce

**2 tablespoonsful *miso* – any variety (preferably
'genmai' brown rice miso)
8 tablespoonsful *tahini* sesame cream
1¾ cupsful water
1½ teaspoonsful grated orange peel**

Mix *tahini*, *miso* and water together and cook in a
saucepan on a low flame for ten to fifteen minutes. Add
orange peel when sauce is done. (For a delicious spread
for sandwiches and bread simply use less water, mix all
ingredients to a buttery paste and do not cook.)

Tamari Sauce

You can substitute shoyu or other good quality soya
sauce for tamari in this recipe. The sauce is also good
with most cooked green vegetables.

**2 tablespoonsful oil
4 tablespoonsful *tamari*
¼ cupful water
1 tablespoonful arrowroot or *kuzu* (Japanese
arrowroot)**

Mix *tamari* and oil in a small saucepan and bring to the
boil. Add water and boil for five minutes. Meanwhile
dissolve arrowroot in two tablespoonsful of water and
add this mixture to the boiling liquid mixture. Stir
constantly until the sauce thickens.

Raisin Sauce

Raisin sauce is not only good with rice (i.e. when serving curries, or to stimulate the interest of children) but also goes well over vegetables such as steamed carrots. A bit of zest, grated lemon peel, can be added if desired.

3 tablespoonsful oil
3 tablespoonsful wholewheat flour
1 cupful fresh apple juice or apple juice concentrate
rediluted with 6 parts water
1 cupful chopped raisins or whole currants
¼ teaspoonful sea salt

Heat the oil in a saucepan, then add the flour and roast for a minute, stirring continuously. Slowly add the apple juice, taking care lumps do not form. Cook slowly, stirring frequently, until the sauce has thickened. Add raisins and simmer gently for four minutes, stirring regularly to prevent sticking.

Mushroom Sauce

3 tablespoonsful oil
3 tablespoonsful wholewheat flour
1 cupful water (or milk in some proportion for a
richer sauce)
2 teaspoonsful soya sauce
¼ cupful chopped mushrooms

Sauté mushrooms in oil for a few minutes, then add the flour. Cook for a further minute, stirring continuously. Slowly add the water stirring constantly, adding more water carefully to avoid forming lumps. When the sauce has thickened, add tamari to taste.

You can adjust the thickness of this sauce by increasing the amount of flour and oil used.

Savoury Thickened Tamari

This is a dipping sauce and is very popular in Japan. It is delicious used as a dip for finely slivered carrots, spring onions, celery etc. Also poured over cooked vegetables, tofu, or cooked rice.

1 teaspoonful sesame oil
¼ cupful soya sauce
¼ cupful water
1½ tablespoonsful *kuzu* (dissolved in a little water)

Heat a small pan and coat with the oil, then add the soya sauce and bring to the boil. Add the water and dissolved *kuzu*, bring to the boil and then simmer gently stirring constantly until the sauce is thickened.

Tomato Sauce

Serve in the middle of a bowl of rice.

3 tablespoonsful olive oil
2 medium chopped onions
5 cloves garlic
2 stalks celery
1 can tomato *purée* or *purée* of 4 peeled and seeded
tomatoes
¼ teaspoonful thyme
1 teaspoonful soya sauce
1 tablespoonful vinegar
3 umeboshi plums, pitted

Sauté vegetables, garlic, thyme, soya sauce, vinegar and plums. Add *purée* diluted with equal quantity of water. Simmer gently for 15 minutes.

Pesto Sauce

**1 large bunch of fresh basil
4 cloves garlic
$\frac{1}{2}$ cupful of pine nuts
$\frac{1}{2}$ cupful of grated parmesan cheese
2 oz (50g) olive oil**

Pound the basil leaves (removing the stalks) in a mortar with garlic, a pinch of salt and the pine nuts. Add the cheese. When the pesto is a thick *purée*, add the olive oil a little at a time, stirring constantly. The finished sauce should have the consistency of a creamed butter. If it is impossible to get fresh basil, parsley may be used instead and walnuts instead of pine nuts, but it will of course have a completely different flavour, although still delicious.

Cauliflower Sauce

**1 cauliflower
2 medium onions, chopped
3 tablespoonsful flour
4 tablespoonsful oil
1 pint (550ml) water
1 teaspoonful salt
1 teaspoonful *tamari***

Clean cauliflower and lightly cook in boiling water. Drain and reserve liquid. *Sauté* onions in the oil and when transparent stir in the flour. Cook lightly for a moment or two and then add the pint (550ml) of water (using the cauliflower stock). Stir until the sauce comes to the boil. Add the cauliflower, well broken up. Season with salt and *tamari*, then turn down to a very gentle heat and cook slowly for 20 minutes. Serve over rice or any grain.

Rice Soup

1 cupful chopped onions
1 cupful rice
pinch each of thyme, marjoram, salt
bay leaf
4 pints (2.3 litres) boiling water
1 tablespoonful *tamari*
1 cupful chick peas or haricot beans, pre-cooked

Sauté first six ingredients till onions are transparent. Add boiling water and pressure cook for 30 minutes. Push through strainer. Add *tamari* and pre-cooked chick peas or haricot beans.

Rice, Vegetable and Tofu Soup

1½ tablespoonsful oil
1 stalk celery, diced
1 carrot, diced
4 mushrooms, thinly sliced
1 cupful brown rice
3 cupful vegetable stock
1 teaspoonful grated ginger
1½ tablespoonsful soya sauce
¼ teaspoonful salt
2 teaspoonsful *kuzu*, dissolved in a little water
6 oz (175g) *tofu*, cut into small cubes

Sauté the celery, carrots and mushrooms in the oil for five minutes or until tender. Set aside. Mix the stock, rice, ginger and soya sauce together. Bring to the boil and stir in the *kuzu*. When thickened, stir in the vegetables and the *tofu*. Bring back to the boil and serve immediately.

Blended Rice and Onion Soup

**1 tablespoonful oil
2 cupsful pre-cooked rice
1 large onion, finely chopped
2 tablespoonsful oatflakes
1 pint (550ml) water
1 tablespoonful soya sauce
parsley, finely chopped**

Sauté the onion in the oil until transparent. Add the rice, oatflakes, and water and bring to the boil. Simmer for 20 minutes. Stir in the soya sauce then blend in the blender. Serve sprinkled with chopped parsley.

Lemon Soup

**2¼ pints (1 litre) vegetable stock
3 eggs
1 cupful cooked long grain brown rice
1 lemon
soya sauce**

Heat the stock to boiling and add cooked rice. Remove from heat. Juice the lemon and beat the juice with the eggs, diluting this mixture with a little of the stock. When the mixture is smooth, combine with the stock and cook gently for two to three minutes. Do *not* bring to the boil. Season with soya sauce and serve.

6
SALADS

Salads based on brown rice are particularly ideal in summer but they are delicious at any season. Apart from being a useful way of preparing left-over cooked rice, salads also make a welcome change from packed lunches when cheese sandwiches have begun to pall.

CLIVE BIRCH

Mixed Bean Salad

4 oz (100g) dried kidney beans
4 oz (100g) chick peas
4 oz (100g) haricot beans
4 oz (100g) brown rice, cooked
1 lb (450g) sliced green beans
2 onions

Vinaigrette:
1 cupful olive oil
½ cupful wine vinegar
crushed clove garlic
salt and pepper
mustard

Soak pulses overnight, then cook for 1½-2 hours –
separately if convenient. Cook green beans in salted
water till tender but not too soft. Slice onions into rings.
Drain beans and green beans as well. Mix in a bowl with
onions and pour on vinaigrette. Cool.

Brown Rice and Lentil Salad

This delicious salad is at its best with *lentilles de Puy*, the delicious small green lentils from France. There is a Canadian lentil that is similar, and of course you can use the usual greenish grey 'continental' lentils with good results.

1 cupful brown rice
1 cupful lentils
1 cupful sliced mushrooms
¼ cupful chopped spring onions
½ green pepper, chopped
1 heaped tablespoonful chopped walnuts
¼ cupful chopped and peeled cucumber
3 tablespoonsful chopped parsley

Dressing:
5 tablespoonsful oil
5 tablespoonsful vinegar
1 teaspoonful mustard powder
2 cloves garlic, crushed
¼ teaspoonful fresh-milled pepper
1 teaspoonful soya sauce

Cook the lentils in four parts boiling water until soft (about ¾ hour) without salt. Cook the rice in lightly salted water until done. Combine lentils and rice and pour the salad dressing over this mixture while it is still warm. Cool. Add rest of ingredients and garnish with parsley sprigs or slices of tomato or pimento.

Rice Salad

**8 oz (225g) rice
1 teaspoonful turmeric
¼ red pepper
8 oz (225g) tomatoes
1 small tin sweet corn
2 sticks celery**

Dressing 1
**juice of 1 lemon
½ teaspoonful paprika
2 tablespoonsful chopped parsley
salt and pepper
4 tablespoonsful olive oil**

Dressing 2
**¼ pint (150ml) plain yogurt
salt and pepper
mustard
1 teaspoonful soya sauce
1 clove garlic
pinch cayenne pepper**

Cook rice. Skin and chop tomatoes. Finely chop pepper and celery sticks. Mix dressing ingredients. Stir rice and vegetables into dressing 1 and press into mould. Refrigerate for twelve hours. Turn out onto a bed of lettuce and serve with dressing 2.

Paradise Salad

3 cupsful rice, cooked – long and short grain mixed
4 sticks celery, diced
2 oz (50g) raisins
fresh herbs, chopped
2 oz (50g) grapes
1 tablespoonful parsley, chopped
4 tomatoes
4 hard-boiled eggs
1 cupful mayonnaise
8 black olives

Mix the cooked rice with the celery, raisins, any fresh herbs available and grapes. Place in a mould in the middle of a serving dish arranging the halves of tomato and egg alternately. Put a teaspoonful of mayonnaise onto each egg half and an olive onto each tomato half.

Almond and Rice Salad

2 cupsful rice, cooked
$\frac{1}{4}$ teaspoonful curry powder
$\frac{1}{2}$ cupful mayonnaise
$\frac{1}{4}$ cupful celery
$\frac{1}{2}$ cupful almonds, toasted and slivered

Chill the rice and stir in the rest of the ingredients. Serve at once.

Adzuki Bean Salad

2 cupsful rice, cooked
4 oz (100g) adzuki beans
1 large green pepper, chopped and de-seeded
2 stalks of celery, finely chopped
½ cucumber, diced
6 spring onions, chopped

Dressing:
4 tablespoonsful olive oil
1 tablespoonful wine vinegar
1 clove garlic, crushed
1 teaspoonful mustard
1 teaspoonful salt
2 tablespoonsful parsley, finely chopped
2 tablespoonsful celery, finely chopped
freshly milled black pepper

Soak beans overnight. Then cook until tender (about an hour). Do *not* add salt. Mix the dressing in a salad bowl. Add the cooked rice and beans straight into the dressing. Turn lightly with a fork and leave to cool. Mix in the chopped vegetables. Taste and season with salt and pepper.

Irish Salad

**2 leeks, well cleaned and finely shredded
4 pieces celery, finely chopped
8 oz (225g) carrots, peeled and grated
1 cupful cooked brown rice**

Dressing:
**3 tablespoonsful olive oil
1 tablespoonful wine vinegar
1 clove garlic
½ teaspoonful mustard
salt and pepper
finely chopped parsley
12 black olives**

Mix vegetables in a salad bowl. Mix dressing and add to vegetables. Garnish with the parsley and olives. Serve with warmed wholewheat bread.

Greek Hot Rice Salad

**2 cupsful hot brown rice, cooked
1 teaspoonful salt
¼ teaspoonful pepper
1 onion, finely chopped
¼ cupful olive oil
1 tablespoonful lemon juice
oregano
parsley sprigs and ripe olives for garnishing**

Add, salt, pepper and onion to the hot rice. Mix the oil and lemon juice and pour over the rice. Sprinkle with oregano and toss lightly. Garnish and serve at once.

Pink Rice Salad

1 cupful finely chopped celery
1 cupful finely chopped parsley
1 cupful pre-cooked, diced and cooled beetroot
3 cupsful long grain brown rice
1 cupful pre-cooked, diced and cooled carrots

Mix above ingredients in a bowl.

Dressing:
4 tablespoonsful olive oil
1 tablespoonful vinegar or lemon juice
salt
freshly ground pepper
1 tablespoonful *tahini*

Mix ingredients together. Pour over salad. Mix well until beet juice stains rice pink, taking care salad does not become mushy.

7
RISOTTOS,
CASSEROLES
AND RISSOLES

Casserole Vert

**1 chopped onion
2 cloves garlic, crushed
oil
2 cupsful cooked brown rice
¾ cupful grated cheddar cheese
2 beaten eggs
2 cupsful milk
1 tablespoonful soya sauce
½ cupful chopped parsley**

Sauté the onion and garlic in oil until onions are soft. Mix remaining ingredients together and add the onions and garlic. Pour into a casserole dish and bake at 350°F/180°C (Gas Mark 4) for at least half an hour or until it has set.

Autumn Risotto

4 tablespoonsful olive oil
1 large onion, chopped
2 large cloves garlic, crushed
2 potatoes, diced
2 carrots, diced
3 courgettes, sliced across
8 oz (225g) string or green beans, chopped
4 oz cabbage, shredded
2 cupsful brown rice
2 cupsful vegetable stock
2 cupsful tomato juice
2 tablespoonsful parsley, chopped
salt and pepper
1 cupful Parmesan cheese

Heat oil until hot in heavy casserole. Add all the vegetables stirring constantly until they begin to soften. Add the rice, stir and cook for a further few minutes before adding the stock and tomato juice. Now add the garlic and season with salt and pepper. Bring to simmering point then transfer uncovered to the oven for 35 minutes at 350°F/180°C (Gas Mark 4). Remove and sprinkle with Parmesan and parsley and leave to stand for ten minutes in a warm place before serving.

Tasty Casserole

2 cupsful long grain brown rice
1 red pepper, chopped
1 green pepper, chopped
4 oz (100g) mushrooms, chopped
2 onions, chopped
1 carrot, chopped
4 oz (100g) peas
1 tablespoonful curry powder
1 teaspoonful black pepper
1 pint (500ml) vegetable stock, boiling
2 tablespoonsful lemon juice

Gently cook the onions in lemon juice. Add the rice and curry powder and stir over heat for a few minutes. Put rice mixture in a casserole dish and add the peppers, mushrooms, carrots, peas and black pepper. Add the stock, stir well and cover. Bake in a 350°F/180°C (Gas Mark 4) oven for one hour.

Cashew Risotto

2 cupsful cooked brown rice
4 oz (100g) chopped cashews or chopped almonds
2 tomatoes, peeled and seeded
2 hard-boiled eggs, chopped
2 tablespoonsful parsley, chopped
½ lemon
soya sauce
wholewheat breadcrumbs
3-4 tablespoonsful grated cheese

Finely grate the lemon rind and juice the lemon. Mix juice, rind, rice, nuts, tomatoes, eggs and parsley, seasoned with soya sauce. Place mixture in an oiled casserole dish. Sprinkle top with mixed breadcrumbs and cheese. Bake at 300°F/150°C (Gas Mark 2) for 20-25 minutes.

Rice, Rye and Vegetable Pie

1 cupful carrots
1 cupful parsnips
1 cupful cabbage
2 cupsful pre-cooked rice and rye, mixed
1 cupful grated cheese
1 teaspoonful arrowroot

Sauté carrots, parsnips and cabbage, then cover, adding a cupful of water and simmer for 15 minutes. Season with *tamari* and thicken by stirring in a teaspoonful of arrowroot mixed to a smooth paste with water. Add two cupsful of rice and rye and grated cheese. Line pie dish with dough. Fill with mixture and cover with lid and bake till pastry is cooked.

Sunshine Risotto

This delicious dish combines the nutty flavour of toasted seeds with the sweetness of dried fruits to give an exotic flavour and a satisfying meal. Dried fruits featured heavily in the cuisine of the Middle Ages in conjunction with game and cereal dishes. The traditional English breakfast of 'frumenty' was made with boiled wheat, a little milk and 'Raisins of Corinth' (as currants were known in their early days when they were the most commonly available dried vine fruit). Nowadays fruit packers often treat raisins, sultanas and currants with paraffin oil to speed up the rate at which they can be packed, but this is undesirable as paraffin can inhibit the digestive system's ability to absorb the nutritive elements in your food. Dried fruit which has been rewashed and cleaned and repacked, unoiled, is available for a few pence extra per pound at many natural food stores and other outlets.

1 cupful roasted sunflower seeds
1 carrot, diced
2 onions, chopped
3 stalks celery, chopped
vegetable oil
3 cupsful cooked long grain brown rice
¼ cupful currants
½ cupful raisins
1½ cupsful grated cheese
(double Gloucester or Leicester)
1 teaspoonful *tamari*

Sauté the vegetables in oil until the onions are soft and translucent. Mix the seeds and toast in a 350°F/180°C (Gas Mark 4) oven for seven to eight minutes. Remove from oven and *sauté* with the vegetables for two minutes. Add the rice and the raisins and currants, adding a little water if needed to prevent the rice sticking while it heats up. Put the whole mixture into a casserole and mix with half a cupful of cheese and tamari. Sprinkle the remaining cupful of grated cheese over the top and cover. Bake for about ten minutes at 350°F/180°C (Gas Mark 4) until the cheese is melted and just crisping at the edges of the dish.

Onions Farci

The amount of rice used in this recipe depends upon the internal volume of the onions you are stuffing.

4 large onions with outer brown skin removed
1½ cupsful cooked brown rice (approx.)
3 tablespoonsful oil
4 oz (100g) chopped mushrooms
4 oz (100g) double Gloucester cheese, grated
1 tablespoonful soya sauce
1 teaspoonful thyme
fresh milled pepper

Cook the onions in boiling water until tender, at least ½ hour. Drain. Slice off tops and scoop out centres, leaving an outer shell about half an inch thick. Chop the onion centres and tops. *Sauté* half the chopped onion in oil with the mushrooms for four minutes. Add the rice, half the grated cheese, and the seasonings. Stir and fry another few minutes. Cover the base of a casserole dish with the rest of the chopped onion and a little water. Fill the onion shells with the stuffing mixture, covering with the remaining cheese. Bake for half to three-quarters of an hour at 350°F/180°C (Gas Mark 4) or until onions are golden in colour.

Rice Croquettes

**3 cupsful cooked short grain brown rice
1 chopped onion
2 cloves garlic, crushed
½ cupful grated cheddar cheese
2 tablespoonsful wholewheat flour
1 beaten egg
breadcrumbs or bran
oil**

Sauté the onion and garlic until golden. Mix with the cooked rice and grated cheese. Mix with flour to a consistency which can be shaped into small patties. Dip into beaten egg, dredge in breadcrumbs or bran (or a mixture of the two). Bake in a medium oven for half an hour and serve with béchamel or *tamari* sauce.

Peanut Rice Supreme

This recipe is derived from one produced by the Georgia Peanut Commission, a body devoted to the theory that if everyone ate more peanuts the world would be free of wars, pestilence, famine and halitosis. From their recipes we tried and enjoyed this one.

3 tablespoonsful oil, groundnut
1 large onion, chopped
2 cupsful celery, chopped
1 cupful peanuts, chopped finely
3 cupsful cooked long grain brown rice
1 lb (460g) cottage cheese
1 cupful diced cooked carrots
$\frac{1}{3}$ cupful peanut butter (old-fashioned style)
4 eggs, beaten
1 tablespoonful soya sauce

Sauté onion and celery in oil until onions are soft. Add all the remaining ingredients and blend together well. Place mixture in a casserole dish, well-oiled (or lined with oiled foil). Bake at 375°F/190°C (Gas Mark 5) for at least an hour. Unmould the baked loaf which should have set, onto a serving platter, removing foil. Serve with mushroom or béchamel sauce.

Stuffed Cabbage Leaves

1 cabbage
1½ cupsful cooked short grain brown rice
1½ cupsful cooked buckwheat
1 large onion, chopped
1 carrot finely chopped
soya sauce
1 cupful grated cheese
1 tablespoonful vegetable oil

Sauté the onion and carrot in oil and mix with the cooked brown rice and buckwheat. Season with soya sauce. (You may add an egg at this stage to bind the filling if desired.) Stir in grated cheese.

Boil the head of cabbage in water for four to five minutes, then remove from the water and drain. Peel off the outer leaves slowly, taking care not to tear them. Place three tablespoonsful of filling on each leaf, and roll it up tucking in the ends as soon as one complete turn is completed. Oil an ovenproof casserole dish and place the rolls in it side by side. Cover the bottom of the dish with a little water and cover with lid. Bake for 25 minutes in a medium oven, about 350°F/180°C (Gas Mark 4). The rolls should hold together when done and can be eaten hot or cold.

8
ORIENTAL
RECIPES

Brown rice is the traditional staple diet of the countries of the East and it was not until the advent of colonialism and rice polishing that white rice became a popular food of 'advanced' civilization. Even among the Asian community in Britain consumption of brown rice is practically non-existent and a prejudice against it as the food of peasants will take a long time to disappear.

The pantheons of the early religions of many Eastern countries included a deity whose sole responsibility lay in ensuring a rice harvest of ample quantity and good quality, and perhaps also to ensure successful preparation of some of the recipes listed here.

Preparing Sushi

1   sushi mat
     vegetables
     rice
     nori

2   cut into slices

3   serve cold

Sushi

For *hors d'oeuvres*, picnics and the lunchbox, sushi is a delightful way to combine brown rice and vegetables with the goodness of seaweed. To be successful with sushi you really need a 'sushi mat', made of strips of bamboo strung together. They are sold in Oriental shops and also appear in many hardware shops being sold as place mats. In fact, if you cannot find a genuine sushi mat, a bamboo place mat will do, although try to find one that has not been dyed. You will need soft rice for sushi, so cook with 2½-3 parts water, depending on whether you use a pressure cooker or not.

1¼ cupsful soft rice
¼ cupful grated carrot
2 tablespoonsful chopped watercress
1 sheet nori seaweed

Nori seaweed is a variety of laver which has been dried into flat, paper-like sheets.

Toast the nori seaweed by waving it gently above a low flame – the colour will change and it will crispen slightly. Place a sheet of nori on the sushi mat. Lay a thin layer of rice across half the sheet, and lay the vegetables in a row down the centre of the rice. With wet fingers, and using the mat to keep things even and steady, roll the nori sheet over the rice and filling. This should be one complete turn, using the remainder of the nori to rewrap the rice to make a firm outer skin. Cut into length 1-1½ inches long.

You can vary the vegetable part of the filling, and for a long lasting sushi suitable for camping trips or journeys put a bit of finely chopped umeboshi plum in the centre – it will stay fresh for days. Other variations for filling include chopped parsley, toasted sunflower seeds and currants, or any finely chopped cooked vegetables.

Adzuki Mochi

2 cupsful sweet rice (or brown rice if sweet is not obtainable)
½ cupful adzuki beans
4¼ cupsful water
½ teaspoonful sea-salt
¼ cupful sesame seeds
oil

Pressure cook the rice and beans together. (Bring the cooker up to pressure, then lower flame and cook for three minutes.) Leave pan standing undisturbed for a further half an hour. If you do not have a pressure cooker, boil the beans in a pan with lid, for 30 minutes in 1½ cupsful water. Add the rice and 3½ cupsful more of water and bring back to boil. Cover pan and simmer for 40 minutes. Turn off heat and let stand undisturbed for a further half an hour.

Whilst the rice is still hot, remove about half the mixture and transfer to a food mill. *Purée* the rice until it becomes very soft, and then add to the remaining rice and bean mixture. Add the salt. Wet your hands and knead the mixture until blended (if it is too sticky, keep wetting hands with cold water.)

Shape into little cakes approx. half an inch thick, sprinkle each one with sesame seeds. These can be lightly fried in a heavy skillet brushed with oil until golden or baked for 20 minutes in a moderate oven (turn after ten minutes), or shaped into small balls and deep fried.

Nuts, dried fruits, grated apples etc., can be added to make a sweet dessert mochi either cooked with the rice and beans or added just before cooking. Mochi cakes should be refrigerated if not eaten immediately. Uncooked cakes will keep refrigerated for several days until needed.

Vegetable and Lentil Pilau

2 cupsful lentils, cooked
1 teaspoonful coriander
1 teaspoonful sea-salt
3 cupsful rice, cooked
3 tablespoonsful ghee or oil
1 onion, chopped
4 cloves garlic, finely chopped
6 cloves
1 teaspoonful cinnamon
1 lb (450g) mixed vegetables, chopped
1 teaspoonful ginger
1 teaspoonful black pepper
2 bay leaves
3 tomatoes, quartered
4 oz (100g) spinach or greens, chopped

Fry the onion and garlic in one tablespoonful of ghee until golden. Add the rice and spice and stir fry for five minutes. *Sauté* the chopped vegetables and tomatoes separately in one tablespoonful of ghee until tender. Fry the drained lentils with the chopped spinach in one tablespoonful of ghee for a few minutes. Add all the pre-cooked vegetables to the rice and onion mixture, and stir gently for five minutes. Serve garnished with chopped coriander or parsley.

Yellow Rice Pilau

3 cupsful long grain brown rice, pre-cooked
2 tablespoonsful ghee or oil
2 onions, sliced
½ teaspoonful curry powder
10 peppercorns
4 cloves
1 teaspoonful turmeric
1½ cupsful grated coconut
1 teaspoonful sea-salt
10 almonds, blanched and chopped
10 cashew nuts, chopped

Fry the onions in 1½ tablespoonsful ghee until golden. (Keep a little onion aside for garnishing). Add the rice, spices, coconut, and salt. Stir fry gently until the rice becomes yellow. Fry the nuts and onion in half teaspoonful of ghee and use to garnish.

Chinese Rice

2 cupsful cooked brown rice
1 onion
2 cloves crushed garlic
½ cupful sliced mushrooms
1 cupful bean sprouts
½ cupful shredded cabbage
2 beaten eggs
oil

Sauté onions and garlic in oil for five minutes, then add cabbage, bean sprouts and mushrooms and cook gently retaining some crispness in the bean sprouts.

Cook an omelette with the two eggs and when it is well cooked, slice it into thin shreds. Combine rice, vegetables and omelette shreds, retaining about a quarter of the shredded omelette. Stir and fry for another few minutes and serve sprinkled with retained omelette shreds. Garnish with watercress.

CLIVE BIRCH.

Cauliflower Pilau

3 cupsful rice, pre-cooked
2 tablespoonsful ghee or oil
8 oz (225g) cauliflower sprigs
1 onion, chopped
6 cloves garlic, finely chopped
½ teaspoonful cinnamon
6 cloves
1 teaspoonful ginger
½ teaspoonful paprika
2 teaspoonsful sea-salt
1 teaspoonful cumin
½ teaspoonful garam masala
1 cupful yogurt

Sprinkle the cauliflower with salt and pepper and fry in ghee till they begin to turn golden. Remove from the pan and fry the onion and garlic. Replace the cauliflower and add the spices and rice and stir fry for five minutes. Stir in the yogurt and cook for another few minutes. Garnish with finely sliced onion and tomatoes.

Peas Pilau

3 cupsful long grain brown rice, cooked
2 tablespoonsful ghee or oil
1 onion
4 cloves garlic, finely chopped
¼ teaspoonful ginger
6 cloves
1 teaspoonful cinnamon
½ teaspoonful paprika
1 teaspoonful garam masala
1 teaspoonful cumin
1 teaspoonful sea-salt
1¼ cupsful fresh or frozen peas

Fry the onion and garlic in ghee until golden. Add the rest of the ingredients and stir fry until the peas are cooked. Serve with vegetable curry and yogurt.

Pilau Rice

3 cupsful long grain brown rice, pre-cooked but firm
1 tablespoonful ghee or oil
1 onion, sliced
4 cloves garlic, finely chopped
1 piece ginger, finely chopped
6 cloves
A few pieces of broken cinnamon
¼ teaspoonful paprika
1 teaspoonful garam masala
1 teaspoonful cumin
½ teaspoonful sea-salt
½ cupful water or vegetable stock, boiling
fresh coriander or parsley to garnish, chopped

Sauté half the onion and garlic in a heavy skillet (frying pan) until golden. Add the rest of the ingredients and the rice and stir. Fry until the grains become lightly coloured. Add the water, cover the pan and simmer gently until the liquid is absorbed. Serve garnished with the remaining onion (fried) and parsley.

Beetroot Rice

3 cupsful rice
2 tablespoonsful ghee or oil
1 teaspoonful mustard seeds
1 teaspoonful black pepper
½ teaspoonful cumin
2 onions, chopped
1 large beetroot cooked and diced
½ teaspoonful sea-salt
½ teaspoonful turmeric
Juice of 1 lemon
10 cashew nuts, chopped

Fry the onions in two tablespoonsful of ghee. Add the spices and cook gently for a few minutes. Add the beetroot and salt and mix well with the rice. Sprinkle with lemon juice, garnish with fried cashew nuts and serve hot with yogurt.

Indian Savoury Rice

3 cupsful cooked long grain brown rice
2 tablespoonsful of ghee or oil
1 teaspoonful cumin

Heat ghee in heavy skillet. Stir in rice and cumin.

Spicy Rice

3 cupsful cooked long grain brown rice
½ cupful chopped cashew nuts
½ cupful sultanas
¾ teaspoonful fennel seed
½ teaspoonful cumin
½ teaspoonful fenugreek
½ teaspoonful poppy seeds
½ teaspoonful mustard seeds
1 teaspoonful turmeric
2 tablespoonsful ghee or oil
1 onion, finely chopped
¼ cupful grated coconut

Sauté the onion, nuts, sultanas and coconut in a tablespoonful ghee. Stir in the cooked rice. Fry all the spices in the remaining ghee. Mix into the rice until the grains become yellow. Sesame and caraway can be used for variation.

Coconut Rice

1½ cupsful desiccated coconut
3 cupsful long grain rice, pre-cooked but firm
½ teaspoonful turmeric powder
1 large onion, finely chopped
1 tablespoonful ghee
1 teaspoonful sea-salt
6 cloves
10 peppercorns

Melt ghee in heavy skillet and *sauté* onion lightly until transparent. Stir in the turmeric powder, salt, cloves and peppercorns. Add rice and coconut and fry gently together stirring constantly for ten minutes.

Mushroom Pilau

2 cupsful long grain rice, cooked
1 onion, sliced
1 tablespoonful ghee
1 cupful mushrooms
½ teaspoonful sea-salt
¼ cupful peas
½ cupful water or vegetable stock, boiling

Sauté the onion in ghee until golden. Stir in the rice, mushrooms, salt, peas and add the water. Cover and simmer gently for ten minutes.

9
RICE AND TOMATO DISHES

Brown rice and cooked tomatoes provide a very satisfying harmony of flavours, sweet, piquant, and savoury all at once. Italian and Spanish cuisine in particular owe a great deal to this marriage of flavours.

In the nineteenth century a Colonel Johnson broke a longstanding prejudice against tomatoes by eating one on the steps of the courthouse of his home town in Massachusetts. Doctors were in attendance and several people sought to have him restrained as tomatoes were widely believed to be poisonous and were grown for their decorative value only. In fact tomatoes *are*, like potatoes and aubergines, a member of the nightshade family, which also includes belladonna and *datura stramonium*. The active ingredient of these plants, atropine, can cause delirium but usually just leads to disturbed sleep and dreams. An article in the December 1978 edition of *Scientific American* describes research to breed hybrid tomatoes that are completely free of these alkaloids so they can be enjoyed in limitless quantities by all, even those who are particularly sensitive to vegetables from the nightshade family.

Stuffed Tomatoes 1

8 well shaped firm tomatoes
½ cupful chopped mixed nuts
2 tablespoonsful oil
1 chopped onion
2 tablespoonsful cooked rice
½ tablespoonful chopped mint
1 pinch dill herb
1 pinch salt
1 pinch pepper
3 tablespoonsful butter or margarine
½ cupful vegetable stock or water

Several hours before required, slice tops off tomatoes and set aside.

Carefully remove pith and seeds and discard. *Sauté* the remaining ingredients in oil. Gently fill tomatoes. Replace lids. Place in an oiled casserole dish. Put a dab of butter on each tomato. Pour in the stock. Cover the dish and bake in pre-heated oven at 375°F/190°C (Gas Mark 5) until tomatoes are cooked – about 30 minutes.

Stuffed Tomatoes 2

**6 firm tomatoes
½ cupful cooked brown rice
1 large onion, chopped
1 large stick celery, chopped fine
½ cupful mushrooms, chopped
¼ cupful wholemeal breadcrumbs
soya sauce
thyme
2 tablespoonsful olive oil**

Stand tomatoes on stalk ends and slice off tops at the more pointed end. Scoop out seeds and core with a knife and teaspoon. *Sauté* onions, celery and mushrooms in oil until onions are soft and translucent, then add rice, breadcrumbs, thyme and season with soya sauce. The mixture should be moist. Fill the hollowed-out tomatoes, replace the tops, brush with oil and bake in a hot oven for 15-20 minutes.

Mushroom and Tomato Risotto

2 cupsful long grain brown rice
4 cupsful boiling water
4 tablespoonsful olive oil
1 large onion
2 cloves garlic, crushed
8 oz (225g) small mushrooms, sliced
1 lb (450g) tomatoes, peeled, seeded and chopped
1 teaspoonful thyme
1 teaspoonful oregano or marjoram
1 tablespoonful soya sauce

Sauté half the onion in half the oil and add the mushrooms and *sauté* for another four minutes. Stir in the rice and stir and fry for another two or three minutes. Then add the boiling water and simmer for 40-45 minutes.

In another saucepan *sauté* the remaining onion, adding the garlic after a few minutes. Add the tomatoes and simmer gently until the sauce thickens, about twenty minutes, adding a little water and the soya sauce. Add the herbs a few minutes before removing the sauce from the heat, then combine the sauce with the rice. Cover for ten minutes to allow the flavours to combine and serve.

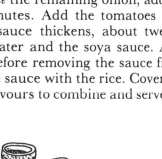

10
DAIRY FOODS

Dairy products combine well with rice, and the bran content of brown rice helps to counteract the digestive sluggishness many people associate with cheesy and milky foods. Yogurt in particular can be added to many of the recipes in other sections of this book, especially rice and cauliflower (see page 68).

Rice and Almond Casserole

2 cupsful cooked brown rice
2 beaten eggs
2 cupsful milk
2 tablespoonsful oil
1 tablespoonful soya sauce
1 cupful chopped lightly toasted almonds (cashew
pieces or chopped toasted hazels can be used instead)

Combine ingredients and pour into an oiled casserole of at least two pints (about one litre) capacity. Bake at 350°F/180°C (Gas Mark 4) until the mixture has set and formed a light brown skin – about 25-30 minutes.

Yogurt Sauce

1 cupful goats milk yogurt
½ cupful chopped chives (other herbs such as parsley, chervil, or fresh basil can be used in place or as well as chives)
1 or 2 cloves garlic, crushed

Mix all ingredients together and serve over hot rice.

Riz Gruyère

For this recipe you can use Gruyère or Emmenthal cheese for that authentic *fondue* flavour, although if you can get a Fribourg or Tomme de Savoie, use it by all means.

2 cupsful sliced onion
3 celery stalks chopped
2 carrots, diced
4 oz (100g) mushrooms, sliced
½ cupful chopped parsley
vegetable oil
2 cloves finely chopped garlic
1 teaspoonful paprika powder
2 teaspoonsful soya sauce
¼ teaspoonful ground ginger
3 cupsful cooked brown rice
1 lb (450g) grated cheese

Sauté the vegetables in oil until the onions are soft. Add the spices and soya sauce. In a shallow casserole, place thin alternate layers of brown rice, cooked vegetable mixture, and grated cheese. Top with grated cheese. Bake for half an hour at 350°F/180°C (Gas Mark 4).

Stilton Salad

While Stilton features in the title of this recipe, Roquefort, blue Wensleydale or even a blue Danish cheese can be used. If you pressure cook the rice, use less water.

3 tablespoonsful olive oil
1 cupful long grain brown rice
2 cupsful boiling water
1 large onion, chopped coarse
1 clove garlic, chopped
1 sweet apple
3-4 cupsful crumbled Stilton

Dressing:
3 tablespoonsful oil
1 tablespoonful lemon juice or cider vinegar
1 clove garlic, crushed

Sauté the onion and clove of garlic in oil until soft and translucent. Add rice and stir and fry for a couple of minutes. Combine with water and simmer for 30-35 minutes or until water is absorbed. Mix with dressing and leave the rice and dressing mixture to cool. When it is cold, core and dice the apple and mix apple and cheese with the rice. Refrigerate before serving.

Baked Eggs on a Rice Bed

1 cupful long grain brown rice
1 onion, chopped
6 oz (175g) grated sharp cheese (i.e. mature cheddar)
6 eggs
2 tablespoonsful wholewheat breadcrumbs
oil
salt
soya sauce
fresh-milled black pepper

Sauté onion in oil until soft, then add rice and stir and fry for another three minutes. Cover with two cupsful boiling water and salt or soya sauce to taste and simmer until the water is absorbed. (35-40 minutes).

Oil a casserole dish and fill with cooked rice mixture. Break the eggs over the bed of rice – the yolks will probably break but this is not important. Sprinkle with salt and pepper, then sprinkle with the grated cheese and finally add a thin layer of breadcrumbs. Bake 20-25 minutes at 250°F/130°C (Gas Mark $\frac{1}{2}$). Serve immediately, sprinkled with chopped parsley.

Rice Salad with Mayonnaise

2 cupsful cooked rice
1 cupful peas, cooked
½ cupful celery, finely sliced
½ cupful chopped green onions
½ cupful chopped tomato
½ cupful mayonnaise
½ cupful sour cream
½ cupful sunflower seeds
salt and pepper

Combine rice, peas, celery, onions and tomatoes. Blend mayonnaise and sour cream and stir gently into vegetables. Chill lightly.

11
SWEETS
AND PUDDINGS

Apart from the variations on the theme of rice pudding, brown rice, and the special variety known as sweet brown rice which is grown in Japan and California, forms the base of several other sweet dishes. None of these recipes contain sugar or honey as these sweeteners are only really necessary when the palate has already been jaded by over-use of them.

The natural sweetness of dried fruits, and the rapid effect of saliva enzymes in turning the carbohydrates of rice into dextrins and other natural sugars, produces satisfying sweetness and a marriage of flavours which are not overwhelmed by the dominating sweetness that even a small quantity of sugar introduces.

The advantages of eating a diet that is free of sugar are well-known and can be briefly summarized as: less likelihood of indigestion; more true energy; healthy teeth; good bone development in children; sweet breath; a healthy appetite for food and enjoyment of its flavours; and a greatly reduced likelihood of falling victim to several degenerative diseases, including diabetes, heart disease and liver problems.

Eating sugar effects metabolic changes in the body that lead to a reduction in the body's reserves of B vitamins and minerals and stimulate an artificial sense of appetite for food to replace these losses. It is this excess appetite that contributes at least as much to obesity as the actual carbohydrates consumed in the sugar itself.

There are several natural sweeteners available which do

not disrupt the body's natural balance as dramatically as sugar. Maltose, derived from the malting of grains, usually barley, is a good one, especially used in conjunction with grains. Fruit juice concentrates such as apple juice syrup or boiled raisin juice also enhance desserts and natural sweetness.

Chilled Rice Pudding

1¼ cupsful milk
1½ cupsful water
1 cupful rice
1 cupful sweet rice
¼ cupful almonds, ground
2 tablespoonsful apple concentrate
skinned and roasted whole almonds

Mix water and milk and bring to the boil. Mix the plain
and sweet rice. Stir into the liquid and cover. Cook
briskly for twelve minutes. Meanwhile mix almonds and
apple concentrate and add to the cooking rice. Turn heat
low and simmer for a further 30 minutes. Place into
individual dessert dishes and leave to cool. Decorate with
whole almonds and chill before serving.

Peach Rice

**3 cupsful rice
1 tablespoonful ghee or butter
1 cupful grated coconut
1 lb (450g) peaches, stoned and sliced
10 cashew nuts, chopped
1 tablespoonful sultanas**

Fry the coconut and peaches in the ghee for five minutes. Add the cashew nuts and sultanas and cook for a few more minutes. Stir in the rice and stir fry until hot.

Brown Rice and Yogurt Supreme

**1¼ cupsful cooked brown rice
8 oz (225g) plain yogurt
1 cupful crushed pineapple (well drained)
2 bananas, diced**

Combine all the ingredients. Chill well before serving.

Rice and Carrot Pudding

If you wish, substitute an equal weight of cooked pumpkin for the carrots.

**2 cupsful cooked carrots
1 cupful cooked brown rice, short grain
¼ cupful fresh apple juice
1 tablespoonful apple juice concentrate, barley malt
syrup or rice syrup
2 tablespoonsful hot oil
pinch each of nutmeg, cinnamon and grated ginger
1 beaten egg
½ cupful currants or raisins**

Purée carrots and add all ingredients. Mix thoroughly adding more apple juice if needed. Bake in an oiled baking dish at 350°F/180°C (Gas Mark 4) for 30-40 minutes. (Place the baking dish in a larger pan with one-inch depth of water to prevent scorching when in the oven).

Brown Rice and Apricot Layer Pudding

**4 cupsful pre-cooked rice
2 cupsful dried apricots (soaked for at least three
hours beforehand)
½ pint (275ml) milk
1 teaspoonful apple concentrate
½ cupful roasted almonds, slivered
1 teaspoonful cinnamon**

Lay one cupful pre-soaked apricots on the bottom of a
casserole dish. Spread two cupsful of rice on the top. Lay
one more cupful of apricots on the rice. Lay a final two
cupsful of rice on top of the apricots. Stir a teaspoonful of
concentrate into the milk plus the cinnamon, and pour
the heated milk mixture over the rice and apricots. Bake
at 365°F/185°C (Gas Mark 4) for about 30
minutes. Serve with slivered and roasted almonds
sprinkled on top.

Rice Pudding

**4 cupsful pre-cooked sweet rice
1 cupful raisins
2 cupsful milk
1 teaspoonful mixed spice
1 teaspoonful nutmeg
1 cupful coconut, desiccated**

Mix all ingredients together and bake in a deep dish at
450°F/230°C (Gas Mark 8).

12
BROWN RICE AND FASTING

One of the greatest factors that has led to the widespread consumption of brown rice is the spread of the macrobiotic way of eating in the United States and Europe in the past decade. The macrobiotic philosophy, based on the dialectical principle of Yin and Yang, enables a person to judge the correct balance of his eating without recourse to calorie charts or lists of mineral and vitamin contents of food.

The macrobiotic diet is primarily a preventive and positive diet, seeking to maximize the mental and spiritual potential of the individual through maintaining a body that, through good diet and regular activity, is functioning at the peak of its capabilities. However, few people can carry through the transition from a conventional diet based on processed refined foods, with sugar and chemical additives without being drawn back to eating habits that not only undermine the body's efficiency but also lead to ill health.

As a means of enabling the body to repair itself George Ohsawa, the founder of modern macrobiotic philosophy, introduced Diet Number Seven, a diet based solely on brown rice which enabled the body's natural cleansing functions to work free of any input of rich and unbalancing foods whilst still maintaining a fundamental level of balanced nutrition. Much disease originates in intestinal malfunction which results in poor blood quality, and, by restoring intestinal motility and effectiveness, the brown rice diet can lead to a cure of many chronic conditions.

Many people have experienced fasting over a period of a week or more and have realized that after an initial difficult period, going without food is not a very distressing process. With practice, fasting becomes much easier and fast days and other variations on fasting themes are a traditional feature of all the world's religions.

A fast using brown rice is an easy way of enjoying all of fasting's benefits without having to do without food entirely. It also cultivates an awareness and appreciation of the advantages of careful chewing, enhances one's enjoyment of the flavour of brown rice, and leads to a greater understanding of the role of rice and other whole cereals as the fulcrum in balancing one's nutrition.

It is not advisable to eat a diet based exclusively on brown rice for more than a few days at the outset, and one should not exceed a week on the diet without good reason, preferably with medical consultation. Case histories are available of individuals who have obtained remission of cancer and other diseases using a brown rice based regimen in a booklet called *A Dietary Approach to Cancer* (available from East-West Centre, 188 Old Street, London EC1).

A brown rice fast can include small amounts of the following foods: sea salt used in preparation of the rice; *gomasio* sesame salt; *tamari* soya sauce; and *tahini* sesame seed cream. *Gomasio* is made by combining eight parts of lightly toasted sesame seeds with one part of sea salt and grinding them together either in a pestle and mortar or a pepper mill. Ready-made *gomasios* are available from many natural food shops, but they lack the flavour of the freshly made condiment. Drinks should be limited to mineral water and herbal teas.

A rice gruel can be made by adding water to cooked rice to the desired consistency and this, lightly seasoned with soya sauce or gomasio, is an ideal way of getting invalids to take food, as well as being a variation to include in a brown rice fast.

Always remember, unless you are used to fasting, the effects not only on your metabolism but also your psyche can be unbalancing at first and care should be taken not to overtax oneself or to engage in activities that call for one's full concentration such as operating machinery or driving a car.

Preparing Brown Rice for Fasting

Sesame Rice. Lightly toast whole sesame seeds in an unoiled frying pan. Stir into the rice, about one tablespoonful of seeds per cupful of cooked rice.

Umeboshi Rice. De-stone a few umeboshi plums and break up the flesh of the plum into four or five pieces and scatter over the rice before cooking. Use no salt in preparing the rice as there is an adequate amount in the plum.

Miso Rice. Dissolve a teaspoonful of miso soybean paste in each cupful of water used in preparing the rice. Boil the rice in the usual way. If you are pressure cooking the rice use one third less miso per cupful of water. Miso, tamari, or shoyu soya sauce can also be added after cooking the rice, but the flavour infuses the grains if added before cooking. In using these remember not to add any salt before cooking.

Herb Rice. You may wish to include a specific herb in your diet such as parsley, mugwort, thyme, etc. When the rice is cooked, stir in a teaspoonful or so of the herb and allow to stand for another ten minutes. The steam and heat of the rice will draw out the herbal flavours. Adding herbs before cooking will lead to overcooking the herbs and either losing their flavour or, in some cases, drawing out a bitter element that is not desirable.

Raw Rice. For intestinal problems, and particularly for purging intestinal parasites, a handful of raw rice eaten as the first food of the day, and chewed very thoroughly, can be very effective. Raw food is always beneficial to the digestive system as it is assimilated farther down the intestines than cooked food, and raw grains in small quantities can be very effective in restoring tone and vitality to this important organ.

Raw rice can also be lightly roasted until slightly browned in colour for a nuttier flavour.

INDEX